THE
RINGING ROCK

Scottish Contemporary Poets Series
Other volumes in this series include:

Gerry Cambridge, *The Shell House*
Jenni Daiches, *Mediterranean*
Kenneth C Steven, *The Missing Days*

THE
RINGING ROCK

Valerie Gillies

Illustration by Will Maclean

SCOTTISH CONTEMPORARY POETS SERIES

SCOTTISH CULTURAL PRESS

First published 1995
by Scottish Cultural Press
PO Box 106, Aberdeen AB9 8ZE
Tel: 01224 583777
Fax: 01224 575337

British Library Cataloguing in Publication Data
A catalogue record for this book is available from the British Library

ISBN: 1 898218 36 6

The publisher acknowledges subsidy from the Scottish Arts Council
towards the publication of this volume

Printed and bound by
BPC-AUP Aberdeen Ltd, Aberdeen

Contents

Valerie Gillies has been writing poetry since she was fourteen, and *The Ringing Rock* is her fifth solo collection.

She also teaches creative writing in schools, colleges and hospitals, and has held writing fellowships in Dundee and the Lothians. She broadcasts and writes for radio and television.

She enjoys working with visual artists and musicians, and has been involved in several original projects recently, including a travelling exhibition by two poets and two artists, following the Tay from source to sea.

Valerie lives in Edinburgh with her husband, children and animals.

Acknowledgements

Acknowledgements are due to many visual artists with whom I have worked recently, especially Will Maclean, Elaine Shemilt, Derek Robertson and Iona Montgomery.

Poems from *Tay Journey* first appeared in the McLellan Galleries, Dundee, along with the poetry of Harvey Holton and the paintings of Douglas Robertson and Angus McEwan, in our *River Spirits* exhibition.

I thank the staff of the National Museums of Scotland for their help, and I am grateful to the memory of Sir Daniel Wilson, who returned the Coygerach from Canada to Scotland.

I would like to thank Savourna Stevenson for her music, and Walter Elliot for his knowledge of the land.

I often think of Jess (Ballagan Joyous) 1978-1993, who was the first to hear many of these poems out of doors.

GENIO TERRAE CALEDONIAE

to the spirit which watches over the land of Caledonia

Part One

THE RINGING ROCK

THE RINK

Light plays on the Rink,
on birches in the broch, its outer wall.
You are here with me in silence.

A doe hare comes this way, in no hurry,
not expecting to find humans here,
loping close enough to touch.

Her warm brown back blends
with the feather-grass, her fur
a burr-elm of reds and yellows.

After her come two jack hares,
one solid, one spindly, following her trail
with twists and turns, tides to her moon.

Most marvellous, moving smoothly,
the run of the hares is the lie of the land.
There are times when the creature is a ghost.

We think they have all gone,
till we turn and look behind us:
in the shadow of a shadow

a golden hare rests in the birchwood,
touched thousands and thousands
of times by the sun.

A SAPLING GREYHOUND

I like to meet my friend the greyhound:
for her, I hang my head upside down
and she takes my ear in her white teeth.
I feel the bite of winter nip the heath.

THOSE RINGING ROCKS

Those ringing rocks, I want to go to one:
It sounds cool, maybe scary for some,
But I would like to hear it.
I'd strike it with another bit
Of stone, to give the rock a voice
And find out why it makes that noise.
My bristling hair would stand on end
At the first note on its wavelength.

THE KING'S FISH
for Will Maclean

Shark in the shallows,
over weedy sandbanks
the spur dogfish swims, unseen
by rowers above the oarweed forest.

Hook in the maw,
hook in the lip,
two hooks, a king's and a hero's,
where it takes the bait quietly.

Its weight lies
on the handline,
Fionn strikes when he feels a bite,
hauls in a sandshark of stinging spines.

The dogfish is prized,
its skin dried
for precious properties, rubbed up
the wrong way, makes a non-slip swordgrip.

Two figures quarrel,
two swordsmen argue
over it till night, while in the sea
dogfishes' eyes are prinkling in the dark.

NOTE: the folktale tells of a dispute between the Viking king and the hero Fionn; both hook the same dogfish and they quarrel over it. The law rules that it is Fionn's fish, because he knew when it first took the bait, and the King goes home to Norway in a rage. Ever since then the dogfish is known as 'the King's Fish', Iasg an Rìgh.

INTAGLIO RINGSTONE
for Walter Elliot

The hill is a globe, and the ploughland,
Well-washed by rainshowers, inswells
Its furrows. Whistling through a blow-hole, can
This be a sea-beast surfacing from where it dwells?

A small and perfect dolphin in the stone
Is leaping, with its tail up,
Smooth-skinned, cut into the two-tone
Slate-grey oval, to fit the sardonyx hump.

This good-luck charm goes as one integer
Fom the engraver's hand, it passes on
By a long-lost man the whole way to its finder.

The beaked dophin makes its own impression:
It scribes the tides, calls and hears underwater,
Crosses seas and bears a man beyond.

*NOTE: An intaglio is a gem with an incised carving. Here, the gemstone is
a sardonyx, with a sunk pattern of a dolphin, lost from a Roman ring and
found at Trimontium by Walter Elliot.*

RETURN OF THE BISON

New flyovers converge on the expressway,
Deepfreeze container fleets competing in their lanes:
I'm surrounded by differences in time and space,
I don't just live in the present, it can change,

I live at all times. Look over my shoulder
At the sliproad, high tech trucks grow animate.
The bison are migrating by a land bridge,
Small groups roaming and returning late.

They make their way through native woods,
They gnaw bark of oak, eat evergreen leaves.
In a sunlit clearing beyond the lay-by,
First out of a dense covering of trees

I see his flank, the more than usual mass
Of a rock outcrop, a boulder with an ear
Flicks as he turns to stare full-face,
A hundred pounds of horn tissue and a beard.

Benevolent beasts, familiar shapes,
The woodland bison have come back;
They browse on aspen suckers in the cities
And all the roads are leafy tracks.

GLEN ESK, ANGUS

A brindled land with native wood,
Birch, alder, rowan and oak,
Fords with flat-topped foothold rocks,
Gravel banks and grassland haughs.

Glen of minerals, brass and tin,
Silver and copper, gold in the linn,
Glen of colours, polar-lights and halo,
Mica-schist rocks and a rainbow.

Illicit stacks, all the whisky stills
Between the burns, worm and malt-kiln.
Broom and heather where hut-circles lie,
Bee-skeps and three kinds of dragonfly.

Who would follow the tawny stream
Has a steep descent into the ravine.
The river saws out a fault-line kerf,
Chasm and cauldron are Esk's cutworks.

Parallel, vertical, walls of true canyon
With seams and veins in a shear zone,
Red jasper, purplish porphyry bands,
Dolerite dykes, bluffs on both banks.

Whisky-toddy currents, torrents and whorls
Contract in narrows, expand in pools,
They move and catch and then converge
Wherever a glen and a mind may merge.

THE WHISKY STILLS

There's a brawl in the Balhangie inn,
the whiff of the Cairncross malt-kiln,
all sticking up, the illicit stacks
behind Glencat, and at the back
of Garelet, behind Carlochy of Lee,
between the burns at Arsallery.

Hidden head of a whisky still
in peat at the summit of Craig Soales,
with ruined bothies up the Kedloch,
far beyond Pool of Fashieloch,
up the Turret, up the White Burn
and on the Shank of Wirren.

They say it was the last store
uncovered at Tarfside in 1904,
but every sample distilled there
perfumes the glen's caller air.
In a broon-pig, whisky pure,
a demi-john of the king of liquor,
'a wee drappie to slocken Sandie'
– no gauger finds his toddy.

BURN NAMES

Where the Branny turns its quern
And Deuchary's a black clay burn,
the Gealet slope is short, abrupt,
Badlessie, the enclosure's tuft,
Bennyglower chatters, clattering sound,
Adedazzle moves deiseal right around.

Burn of Cochlie, place of husks,
Burn of Keenie, deep in moss,
Dalbrack in its dappled dell,
Burn of Bathie, cowbyre's smell,
Burn of Corlick with its stepping stone,
Ademannoch's trout, the monks' own.

Burn of Reehewan is the slope of Ewan,
Corriehausherun's folk run in a band,
But the Waters of Mark and Tarf and Cat
Belong to the clans of Horse, Bull, Wildcat,
Whose totems warn you're in their territory:
They were here and always will be.

SLATERS

The scaffolding is up.
Two slaters sit on a block
facing each other.
They flake and knock
shapes from the grey stack,
raise their hands to chop
at the split-thin plates
with clippers.
Their collars hang loose
at the backs of their necks
like manes.
Now they are winged
with flying slivers
like feathers.
Ready to slate,
they are two confronted,
two griffins at the gate.

THE MASTER GLASSMAKER
for Charles Bray

Blow, blow, you have to blow,
roll the pipe, cut and go,
turn, turn it the other way,
burn the rods,
fuse and overlay.

Breathe in the smell of burning wood,
open the coop, red and good:
fresh sand, you need fresh sand!
Step on it,
hot foot and hand.

Sweep one curve out from the pyre,
glassmaster, drive your furyfire,
work it in the smoke and flame,
let it be,
here you go again.

The glass speaks its own way,
the glass is always a mystery,
you never know what it will do:
talk to the glass,
it talks back to you.

SHALE BINGS

The roads are red, the ground smells raw,
dank soil and air in ironstone country,
the oilshale smelted with coking coal,
bings and farms among rush-choked uplands.

You are the darling place of disused quarries,
dismantled railways, new open-cast mines.
Your rocks, upraised, are worn down again,
buried under the pile of their own ruin.

You lie on the surface of the world,
abandoned on the skin of the earth,
the stacks and jags of red shale
moored among moss-hags and old pits.

You keep bringing up the past.
Motorbike boys are scrambling over the top
when the bing moves beneath them.
A bike turns over: wheels in the drift.

Bings rise and the valley subsides,
fields sink, let down into new hollows,
rimmed with crumbling red cliffs
that creep, change shape under stress.

Over your shake holes and air shafts the wind
enjoys an open channel to the workings
of the mine: it has sought its way in there
and to the workings of the human mind.

OIL COUNTRY

North Lanarkshire
farms waterlogged mire
around oil-extracting
shale bings

A crest
of grass
capping
the bing
a view
as far as the Cleugh
from Wildshaw
to Mountainblaw

I wrote a teenage letter
across this empty quarter
to Thesiger
the great explorer
about his Arabia
how it had a
form and colour
like Lanarkshire

my peaty desert
a dead cert
for his Wadi Andam
in Oman
a sure thing
all rotten grazing
and slaty
beauty
And he wrote back
among the Marsh Arabs of Iraq

Next year I flew over
deserts of rose and ochre
new oil
would despoil

while i was away

you came looking for me
where the deerskin dries on the shed door
and the hound lies out like a rock

you were asking for me
where a steady stream flows past the field
and the rain sounds easy in the grass

you're returning for me
there at night you go by among the trees
and time shifts round like the wind

my jacket

my jacket is the colour
of the oak on the hill
wrists and arms of wood
up to the breast

windcoat
acorn afloat
egg and cup
leathery shuck

in the glade
my cold shoulder
against the trunk
vanishes

oak tree
light canopy
bark placket
cloudjacket

a wavy leaf flickers
on my head
i can't leave
without my jacket

FLY THE LURCHER

Black Fly drifting along the flank of the hill,
you come running now, close in at heel,
to turn up your fox-face, it's new,
the face the fox made for you.

He came to rip sheep, but instead
his jaw snapped shut on your skullhead.
Torn faces and a running fight on the tally,
a cry on the breeze blowing up the valley.
The socket scar grows in silver, crescent on Fly
by night, a new moon rising and a starry eye.

LAMPING

the new fawn bitch
he got from the track in the west
he took her out at midnight
she was running on the lamp
she never saw the tree at all
the fox got clean away
her neck was broken

COCK-SALMON'S WINTER WORDS

On sea-milk I grew full,
   The sea-milk my fountain,
I hardly fed in the river-pool,
   Ascending past the mountain.

The scales' edge ragged on me,
   Scales of pale-eyed salmon
Show ring-growth like a tree
   On the stream's weary phantom.

My back steel-green above,
   Back in the river of birth,
My jaw's hooked curve
   Passes through air's firth.

VIKING BOY

a sandstorm strips the dune
to bare-bones
on a straw mat
over a bed of feathers
the boy lies
a hoop of metal
shelters his head
the shield over his face
the sword by his flank
he has a bone comb
not a yellow hair in it
the bed to soften
the blow to the boy
the shield to hide
his young face
from the sharp scatter
from the first handful of sand

FILMWRAPPED FIELDS

The redbrown earth, acre by acre,
is covered in plastic clingfilm sheeting.
The tissue of lies
cheats the eye.
Polythene surfaces
as watery mirage. One recent artifice
speeds the greedy harvester
but takes away the seasons' meaning.

The sheeted crops sprout,
the film's rolled off before they rot
inside.
What are we thinking about?
Not a lot.
We keep our human pride:
a pig's head preserved, ears, snout
and eyes, in formaldehyde.

AT THE SAND AND GRAVEL QUARRY

The sandbrim is riddled with rabbit holes
on the quarry lip by Loquhariot;
orange cartridge cases tossed down, roll
past a metal pail peppered with pellet-shot.

JCBs work at high speed, excavator-yellow,
gobbling the gravel hills. Beyond,
butterstone against the green hollow,
the pillar-shades and ruined pile of Crichton.

Play Hill behind, where clouds fly
the leap of light, a crack in the sky,
a sunbeam to see Crichton by.

In his eight years here, St Kentigern
constructed a cross of sea sand: discern
traces of it, light and shade crossing in turn.

THE CASTLE OF STARS

Borthwick keep is riding high in the night
Where winds circulate with points of light
While the castellan sleeps with moons and visions
And shooting stars leave their impression.
Through the double tower, twin-faced with ashlar,
The world blows in one battlement and out the other.

A good castle is set here like a planet
Emitting beams from the slits of its parapet.
Starshine fills the valley, overflows
Its brim, and close as coloured globes
The sky is hung with stars above, around.
Cottage lights lie along the haugh grounds.

Below, a glow-worm on a stalk of grass
Shines her cold light, minute and greenish.
And on the same footpath the fallen star
Grows after broken weather, a star-shot medusa
You might suppose has dropped from the clouds
If you see it after rain like a shed slough.

Borthwick becomes the castle of stars,
Gilded with their mark: the enemy's scar
Whose artillery not only hit but smashed
Part of the wall, the bombardment's crash
Radiating fractures till the masonry
Starred like glass, like ice, in rays.

Towers of air, diamond air, in skies
The influence of stars has purified.
You walk out to the ultimate knowe,
To sanctuary as well as to watch-tower:
When the valley curls in like a sleeping hand,
Borthwick's tall shadow leans over the land.

COCKENZIE POWER STATION FROM LONGNIDDRY BENTS

The station generates a new coastline:
Thirty million tonnes of coal-burn
Since its commissioning, three million tonnes
Of fly ash
From spent flue gas
Make four lagoons in its brief lifetime.

These sands, Longniddry bay and bents,
Leave pylons like terrets gathering reins
Of megawatt double-circuit overhead lines.
High chimneys are shafts
On tilt carts
For phantom horses at this distance.

A place filled with the sound of hooves,
Split-second timing of a beach-gallop
When chieftains in their prestige chariots
Displayed the best
Bronze-studded harness,
Two-wheelers, iron tyres' shrunk-on hoops.

They left two rein-rings in this findspot:
Cast bronze, buried on the shore,
Gifts of horse-gear in a hoard,
One ribbed,
One lipped,
In a place they could talk to the gods.

The sun runs out along a draught-pole
Of gold, returning to the yoke.
Our gifts are ash and pall of smoke.
The white mare,
The clean cold firth,
The long rocks are her black colts.

If the gods gave them something, somewhere,
They gave a gift back, at the bents,
Foaming at the bit in impatient moments.
Today's for exercising
Racehorses in a string.
Jockeys in the café sip hot water.

BASS ROCK

The rock punctuates the sealine.
Our boat circles the Bass.
Seals swim beneath us,
pop fruit-machine heads up
three at a time, outstare us.

People press towards them,
lean to starboard all at once.
We lurch below the cliffs.
On their dung-yellow rock,
gannets rest a beak-stab apart.

W.J. Maclean '95   Auchmithie towards the Bell Rock

24

Part Two

TAY JOURNEY

THE SOURCE IN THE SNOW

Crests of snow cornices
overhang the precipice.
The ice that on Ben Lui sits
fits.

But deep in the wintry
socket of the great corrie
the well-eye's rim
brims.

Only the current of the source
over freezing rock can course,
the channel of its rill
fills.

In a white world the one thing
that moves, dark and living,
source to sea connects
flex.

Moss-fed highland river,
fullest in winter,
the water it springs
sings.

FLOATING ISLANDS

A narrow sheet of water lies between
The south shore and those steep bat-rocks
Whose colonies swoop out with echo's flock
Of several words, returning what they mean.
Just where wings and voices pass
In mid-loch, resounding up and down,
New islands form of matted roots and grass
Blown by the wind, a moving ground.

Aquatic plants, the reeds and sedges
Will cast off when the winds prevail,
On buoyant hulls they lightly sail,
Colliding with the shore's worn edges.
They're sometimes there, and sometimes not,
The floating islands of Loch Dochart.

Note to Strathfillan Sequence

Nicknamed 'little wolf', the Celtic Saint Fillan lived in Glendochart in the eighth century, and miraculous powers are attributed to his relics in folk tradition.

His bell and staff were guarded by hereditary keepers known as dewars. Carried at the coronation of King James IV, his staff, the Coygerach, is a masterpiece of metalwork, encasing the original wood. The dewars of the Coygerach emigrated to a backwoods farm in Western Canada in the nineteenth century, and the staff stayed there with them for 60 years but eventually, like his bell which had been stolen by an English antiquary, it returned to Scotland.

Fillan's hand bell had the power of flight and could heal the sick. It was kept in the ruins of his chapel, ready to be used to cure madness. The ritual began with a dip in the Holy Pool and ended after a night spent with the bell placed above the lunatic's head. Saint Fillan's bell and staff can be seen in the National Museum of Scotland.

Now lost, the silver case containing his arm-bone was with Robert the Bruce at the battle of Bannockburn, and the King attributed his victory there to its miraculous appearance on the preceding night.

Today, cures for many illnesses are attributed to Fillan's healing stones, preserved in the mill at Killin for over a thousand years.

THE BELL

Give me a ring
about St Fillan's bell

clang clang clank
the beating bell
like pails
like cowbells
cracked and clappered
rings in your ears
goes right through you
its sounding clangour
its loud *clogarnach*
jangling

the *ronnaich,* the poet-bell
sang songs, rang
to call people
clang clang clank
it cracked on the day
it flew here
it beats all the windy places
it claps time
it has a tongue
rung against thunder
it frees us from danger
by fire or lightning-flash

quadrangular, clang
bronze-clad, clang
dragon-handled, clang
hum tintinnabulum
rung around
its sound creates
its shape hangs
between earth and sky
in the bell-vault
it cures lunatics
the bell flies overhead
a crack of light
rings the changes

cast all in one
hand-bell, mixed metal
though it's carried off
it will return
ringing all the way
grateful to the ear
of the wanderer in the bush
its clang softened by distance
by the intervening forest
its potent *clogarnach*
announces its return
to St Fillan's cell
his yellow bell

THE HOLY POOL

It's dusk and a first quarter moon.
A mad girl shambles on a riverbank
Rotted by rain, splintered by frost,

Wasted by wind and sun. A turf
Loosening, she drops into the water,
Taking a plunge into the holy pool.

At a wide angle of the river,
The pool is broad and deep, so clear
You can see the gravel on the bottom.

Fist full of pebbles, her mouth opens,
She looks up through the water:
Wavy figures are peering down at her.

They walked her thirty miles for this.
Her brothers drag her to the surface
By a rope, tight round her waist.

She bobs like a cork, as mad as ever.
Wet and wistful, she carries her stones
To the three cairns, round the lucky way.

It's all happening in the dark, yes,
Under what could be the moon they walk
The half-mile to the ruined chapel.

Her head centred in the heartshaped stone,
They tie her down, under a wooden frame
Knotted with ropes. Her cries tug,

Covered with straw for the night.
They place St Fillan's bell on her head,
A crazy nightcap on the girl.

Alone, she's hearing the riverwave
Whisper of change in its changes of sound:
The pool, the bell, the bell, the pool.

Damp from her face and hair
Condenses on the sides of the bell
And runs down, bell-metal sweats for her.

Inside the bell is inside the pool.
Someone's drawing on the rope,
Bringing her up through four elements:

Pool where the earth-bank holds water,
Bell where fired bronze holds air.
Her eyes open underwater, under light.

At sunrise her brothers return to lift
Off the bell. They see the knots are loose
That tied her body and warped her mind.

Coda: The Girl Speaks

'My mouthful of water
from the holy pool
I swam in four elements

My mind washed in air
in the shock of the pool
going under St Fillan's Bell

I saw my dead grandfather
return to help me,
he untied the knots

I am a child of grace
in the chapel of marvels
my reason returns

I make my circuit
in the pool, in the bell,
in the fellowship of my Fillan'

THE COYGERACH

Across the Atlantic, you're a wanderer
Shining in silver-gilt, a sea tinker.
    Trapping the bright stick
    Your case becomes holy as its relic.
In your own land you're a stranger.

The metalworker taps in rivets
Round the small hole of your gullet,
    Core for the crook, the crozier
    Encased in bronze here:
This rifled groove could spin a bullet.

Springs of metal turn around the knop,
A charmstone of crystal in the drop
    Tossed in coil and quoit
    One line visits every point
Chased with silver in a wiry rope.

Wood sunk in a hollow, streamy
Eddies in a spate of filigree
    Show sinuous space is dense,
    Make meaning out of emptiness,
Frost on your marvellous tree.

Human arms are carrying
You to the crowning of our Kings.
    Like a girl in her snood,
    You wear your monks-hood,
A cloud aground in your lightning.

Your keepers farmed at Ewich.
A hill with its back up, their relic
    Glittered in a simple croft;
    Shrine with your crest aloft
Like a mountain pony's mane, just as thick.

If your dewar set out on a journey
He had the royal letter, he answered only
To the King, he could pursue
Reivers, pass among tribal feuds
Anywhere in Scotland, that's your potency.

People could ask for the cattle cure
Or one for fever in humans, curlicues
Of water poured through, sprinkled
On them, given them to drink.
Wherever the Coygerach dips, is pure.

River-curve Coygerach, no-one can stand
Too close to your current coming in to land.
Liars lose the power to speak,
Treasure returns with its thief,
You are the light shining from Fillan's hand.

THE NIGHT BEFORE BATTLE

Seeing the wind
before the storm
the king watched Fillan's
miraculous arm
float on its own
through the silver case
till the arm-bone
clakkit into place.

Scotland's pride
at Bannockburn shown,
what mountain hides
his holy bone?
Our saint, our Fillan,
our fate transform,
seeing the wind
before the storm.

THE HEALING STONES

A child goes to Killin in spring
to St Fillan's healing stones,
eight waterworn stones he left us
then we were on our own.

Gather the Christmas rushes
that have been washed up
by floods upon the riverbank,
they must never be cut.

Stones for each part of the body,
for the head and breast and back,
for the limbs and internal organs,
must rest on fresh riverwrack.

There's a black oval curing-stone
against the child's pain.
'Three times one way, three the other,
now the first way again:

rub it lightly around.'
The child's face flushes red,
her body tingles, from icy stone
a sensation of heat spreads.

In place, back on their rushbed,
the stones lie after the spate.
A great flood has swept over them
and over the child, from the saint.

INCHBUIE

The falls roar, I can't hear
The sound of a human voice
Even close up to my ear.
Midstream, the island is a porpoise,

Humpback, in a rock boss.
It's padlocked. I need the key
To walk on the thick gold moss
Of the yellow island of Inchbuie.

It has a path for a spine,
Leading gently up and down
Past lichened beech and pine.
Moss muffles any sound.

Is this island afloat?
Below the graveyard of the chiefs
It ends, sharp as the prow of a boat
Where two branches of the river meet.

The fold of the dead is secure,
Buried on lovely Inchbuie,
Life moves around their enclosure.
Is anybody watching me?

In their vault is a flat slab,
A round hole cut in it, an aperture
Through which the spirit of MacNab
Issues to watch my departure.

The rapids send up a haze.
It was a MacNab in Canada
Who set an American gunboat ablaze
Over the falls of Niagara,

While the twenty-first chief of the clan
Rowed with the flow of the water
To become an Olympic oarsman:
Inchbuie still has its watcher.

Note: Inchbuie is a river island at Killin. The last person buried has to keep watch over the island until the next funeral comes. This is called Faire Chlaidh, *the graveyard watch.*

WATERSPOUTS

Who sees the waterspouts drive over the loch
In long succession, and crash in spray on the crags,
Will brave out the storm on the rock ledge
And be watching in the bield of the western slope.

Who hears the waves spout words from their mouths
Exhaled in a breath, and steam blow out and up,
Will hiss when the winds' voices fly through stone cliffs,
Can go through anything, like a shout passes through rocks.

CRAGGANTOLL

Stripped to the waist, my Angus grandfaither
Was marked like a rock in Strathtay.
Since the great war, he was weathered, brave:
He'd be stropping his cut-throat razor,
I'd see his wound, small fingers in an entry scar.
The sniper among the trees, who hit
By squinting down the sights, sent a bullet
Below his collar-bone to become this puckered star.

Today, at the rock of holes, puzzling
Over its surface honeycombed with pits,
My hand rests on the torso of the boulder.
Here's a cup-mark; I put three fingers in,
I am looking straight up to the summit
Of Ben Lawers, to the storm-scalped shoulder.

THE SPECTRAL HUNTER

Two ornithologists survey
the rocks and trees,
looking down into the valley,
counting species.

A man walking up the Kirkton glen
with an early-morning stride
is seen by both of them
clearly on the hillside.

He has two deerhounds,
leggy, rockhard
tall dogs that bound
and are wire-scarred.

Two hounds of the crags
and a wind-wraith
rousing the stags
in Corrie Chaoraich.

Dogs with leather collars,
the gifts of two mountains,
one given by Meall Reamhar,
one by Meall an Fhiodhain.

He sets his own pace,
headlong streams and rain,
the valley graced
by the hunter again.

All things are caught,
the world is snared
between deer and grey dogs.
He lives on air.

Try the telescope
but he moves on,
from Kirkton's slopes
he is gone.

MACGREGOR'S LEAP, GLEN LYON

two firs planted on either side of the road
two crags facing a twisting stream

between my two ears, the high note of Lyon
the river throttled in the ravine

in rock-cauldrons, boiling kettles
like Will o' Phaup's loup, up Ettrick:

two heroes, two athletes,
artists of the leap

SPUT BAN, PASS OF GLEN LYON

Only for mountain goats, this path
above the Platform Pool, this route
is unsafe: don't use it.

The cross rock of the Pass
which stopped glacial waters once
is channelled and cleft.

Sput Ban is seen through first leaves,
the trees budding bare enough to see
through to the white spout.

Dip my shirt in a south-running stream
and put it wet on me.
The neck of the pool gushes out.

My back against a tree,
my foot against another, hold me
in the hanging wood

high over the gorge
above the drop, the tapping forge
the water's rush includes.

Someone in there
compels my stare
into the river's undertow.

My eyes lift,
rocks rise and shift.
The Sput Ban lets me go.

THE FORTINGALL YEW

North of the kirk,
   Pagan and ivied,
Hollow at heartwood,
   My trunk still alive,

I lay first rings
   While men polish stone,
Part of the primeval forest
   I am not alone.

Thick cords of wood
   Branching in their prime
Spread leaves to the sun
   In Calgacus' time.

Then Stewart clansmen
   Make their best bows,
My hard elastic wood
   Releases their arrows.

Empires rise and fall,
   Wars and polluted seas,
Epidemics, spacewalks,
   Sprigs on my tree.

Though I grow quietly,
   I show in column
How a post of yew
   Outlasts a post of iron.

Boys kindle Beltane fires
   Up against my root,
Splitting apart my trunk:
   I send out new shoots.

From two shells of bole
   Young sprays are fed,
Sable foliage joins in
   One grand leafy head.

In their red wax cups
    Ripen berries, sticky-sweet,
Flesh picked by the thrush
    And poisonous seed.

My twig in your left hand
    Above the widening gap,
The one you speak to hears
    No words but the sap.

I glow in the dark
    With phosphorescent sheen,
Three thousand years
    Rise in dusky green.

Note to Dunfallandy poems

General Archibald Fergusson of Dunfallandy was with the East India Company from 1776 till he returned to Scotland in 1814. He received a sabre-wound on the forehead at the storming of Seringapatam in the Anglo-Mysore war of 1799, where his adversary was the great Tipu Sultan.

WIND HARP, DUNFALLANDY HOUSE

harp at the window
on the turn of the stair
harp at the window
in the currents of air

breath of a spirit
borne on the wind
breath of a spirit
passing through strings

storms tell a secret
from high terrain
storms tell a secret
of corrie and cairn

airwaves harp
shaping the ground
airwaves harp
the land in their sound

SERINGAPATAM, MYSORE STATE

At first, I heard the story from their side.
With Muslim friends on motorbikes
I went to Srirangaputtana for a picnic.
We were students wandering through the fortress,
Hearing it all, the whole citadel on an island,
The sultan no-one could beat, so warlike
He dressed his troops in tiger stripes:
The Tiger of Mysore, our Tipu
Holding off the British, a national hero.
Then the traitor vizier opened a secret passage
And let the enemy in, that judas!

When Tipu was killed, an electric storm
Struck British officers where they stood.
His sons were taken captive, all four,
To make way for the old Raja of Mysore.
They passed through the gate on elephants,
Each boy had a sprig of pearls in his turban
And round his neck an emerald of great size,
With strings of rubies and brilliants.

It seemed impregnable, the fort,
They were up against a bend, a steep slope...
'Why did we wash that fruit in the river?
I think I'm shaking with some fever.'
The back of Ahwad's hand on my forehead:
'No, you're walking where the British put their dead.'
We built a fire on the riverbank. Taking a drum,
The nightwatchman sang a ballad of Tipu Sultan.
Abandoned citadel, deep in the mofussil,
The drumbeat and the sound of jackals.
And in me a horror of its scorched grass,
The slope, the breach, the sense of loss.

A year later, back at home: 'Srirangaputtana?
Thon's the battle of Seringapatam,'
Said Granfaither, 'I've aye thocht
It was whaur your great grand uncle focht,
I hae his cartouche bag and powder horn.
They met wi the braw tiger troops haun tae haun,
In the river an up the brae, wi mony deid.
The hielanders played the pipes in the breach.'

TIPU AND ARCHIE

Athol of knolls and forests, of whitewater rapids,
India of woods and mountains, of wild waterfalls,
As Athol to Karnataka, as Tummel to Cauvery,
Down the mountain passes and out into the strath
Valleys of the Mysore highlands lead into Karnataka,
Snow-fed or monsoon-fed, their rivers are ready.

Tipu Sultan, the Tiger of Mysore, is India's hero,
Archie Fergusson's brow marked with his sabre-scar,
As Athol to Karnataka, as Tummel to Cauvery,
Between the two highlanders there's a similarity:
Days of fortunes made by men who risked everything,
So Tipu to Archie, well-matched adversaries.

It's all foretold on the cross-slab carved here
Where two beasts are fighting, a tiger and a hound,
As Athol to Karnataka, as Tummel to Cauvery,
Where the swimming elephant incised by the Pict
Is the herd crossing Cauvery, gun-batteries six by six,
Tooth to tooth, claw to claw, Tipu to Archie.

Tipu had a full view of the line as it passed,
Seven miles long, looking down on him from the heights:
Stronghold to stronghold, Seringapatam to Dunfallandy.
Now Archie's house on its own bend of the river
Faces a continuous conveyor-belt of sound and colour,
The endless column moving on the dual carriageway.
As Athol to Karnataka, as Tummel to Cauvery,
No Tipu, no Archie disrupts the march today.

MOTHER-OF-PEARL

'Was it all right with your mother
when you phoned? Did you tell her
you'd fallen in the Tay
and that you'd found a pearl?'

'I have a reddish one, and a gray,
but this one is pure white,'
the boy is opening the oyster,
one foot in the wave.

THE SONG OF THE GREYLAG

Sea winds blow
the river flows
geese cross the bight
flying into light

currents shiver
salmon run the river
plunge with quarrons
underwater arrows

lowtide roosts
for the pink-foot
seals haul out
to rest on sandgrout

skein shapes warn
singing the storm
into being
crackling and singing

winging their way
lingering wary
wild spirits tag
along with greylag

TAY SCALES

Carpow cropmarks grow virid,
darken the field with a grid
on the flat-top plateau
the Roman engineers chose.

One find from the fortress
equals a bulletproof vest
or an army flak jacket:
fastened onto fabric

thin plates of sheet-bronze
overlapping in their thousands,
rows fine as fish-scales,
the first coat-of-mail.

Husks for him in harness,
brass of a light cuirass,
scales of butterfly wing
form his covering.

He turns like an armadillo
under a rain of blows
until his scaly shirt
spectacularly bursts.

His shirt awaits repair:
burnished for its wearer,
bound with leather reinforcing
to stop his skin from chafing,

like the river and its banks,
two strips down breast and back,
linen and armour of brass.
Touch and they're scabrous.

Mend them with metal staples.
Now he shines in his scales
like a gilded trout:
on Carpow he'll brazen it out.

ABANDONED BOAT AND ANCHORS

The dinghy is drawn up on shore
like a bathtub full of water

a sandboat sails the bank
a bird with no tail
it leaves no wake

Anchors are left on the beach
like spearheads aimed at stars

sand covers them up to the flukes
birds asleep on one leg
a flock of fists

THE HAND'S SPAN

Your hand places a dram-glass on the board.
Beyond the window, the river is two miles broad.
On the green knuckles of those North Fife hills
My thistledown kiss can seed where it will.

Easier for me to cross the sea-gravel strand
Than reach out now to take your hand.
I steal a glance while you're looking away:
Tides break on a sandbar in the Tay.

Rope-rough, calloused mariner's palm,
Backhand and wrist on the shipwright's arm
Weathering work with bone, resin or strake:
I love every mark your hand makes.

Better for the birds who take wing with a start
Than the two of us who are waking apart.
The river-mouth flows, at one with the land,
It's not so with me and my kiss on your hand.

ESTUARY

'The tide's on the turn here,'
opening the pilot's chart
a man is steering out to sea,

the tiller and the light hand on it
that smells of seawater:
his hand confirms the stars.

PILGRIMAGE

Two years a guest of the river
and the way grows boundless,

the road winding east, downstream,
a wanderer follows waves away.

The shell's your passport, and the staff
will carry you anywhere you wish.

The deep is known by its shell,
the earth by its chosen tree:

coiled shell, born of the waters,
speaks in the mouth or at the ear,

spiral staff, with peeling bark,
moves freely into the sky.

Who'll take the staff and shell
and give it a whirl?

The river buffets blue space
headlong, there's no end to it.